Pterodactyl

Daniel Nunn

Raintree is an imprint of Capstone Global Library Limited, a company incorporated in England and Wales having its registered office at 7 Pilgrim Street, London, EC4V 6LB – Registered company number: 6695582

www.raintreepublishers.co.uk
myorders@raintreepublishers.co.uk

Text © Capstone Global Library Limited 2015
The moral rights of the proprietor have been asserted.

Edited by Daniel Nunn and James Benefield
Designed by Tim Bond
Picture research by Tracy Cummins
Production by Helen McCreath
Originated by Capstone Global Library Ltd
Printed and bound in China

ISBN 978 1 4062 8086 9
18 17 16 15 14
10 9 8 7 6 5 4 3 2 1

British Library Cataloguing in Publication Data
A full catalogue record for this book is available from the British Library.

Acknowledgements
We would like to thank the following for permission to reproduce photographs: age footstock p. 10 (© fotototo); Alamy pp. 8 (© Stocktrek Images, Inc.), 21 (© Corbin17); Corbis p. 18 (© Kevin Schafer); Getty Images pp. 7 (Andrew Kerr), 23 (Ulrich Baumgarten); istockphoto p. 5 (© johan63); Photoshot p. 15 (Raymon Tercafs); Science Source pp. 13 (Roger Harris), 20 (Tom McHugh); Shutterstock 5a (Michael Rosskothen), 5b (Matt Jeppson), 5c (Cathy Keifer), 7 background (mycola), 9 (Space-kraft), 11, 12, 14 (Michael Rosskothen), 16 (Vlada Zhykharieva), 24 (tratong); Superstock pp. 4 (Stocktrek), 6 (Science Photo Library), 17 (Stocktrek Images), 19 (Universal Images Group).

Cover photograph of three Pteranodon Longicepts flying, with two diplodocus dinosaurs near the shore with permission of Shutterstock (Linda Bucklin).

Back cover photograph of pterodactyl reproduced with permission of Shutterstock (Michael Rosskothen).

We would like to thank Dee Reid and Nancy Harris for their invaluable help in the preparation of this book.

Every effort has been made to contact copyright holders of material reproduced in this book. Any omissions will be rectified in subsequent printings if notice is given to the publisher.

Contents

Meet the pterodactyls

Pterodactyls lived long ago.

They are also called pterosaurs.

pterodactyl

snake

crocodile

lizard

Pterodactyls were reptiles.
Snakes, crocodiles and lizards
are reptiles that live today.

Pteranodon

Some pterodactyls were big.

Pteranodon was big.

Pterodactylus

There were other types of pterodactyls. Pterodactylus was small.

What were pterodactyls like?

wings

Pterodactyls had wings.

Pterodactyls could fly.

legs

Pterodactyls had four legs.

Pterodactyls could walk.

beak

Pterodactyls had long beaks.

Pterodactyls ate fish, insects and small animals.

teeth

Some pterodactyls had teeth.

Some pterodactyls did not
have teeth.

Where are pterodactyls now?

Pterodactyls are extinct. There are no pterodactyls alive now.

All the pterodactyls died long ago.

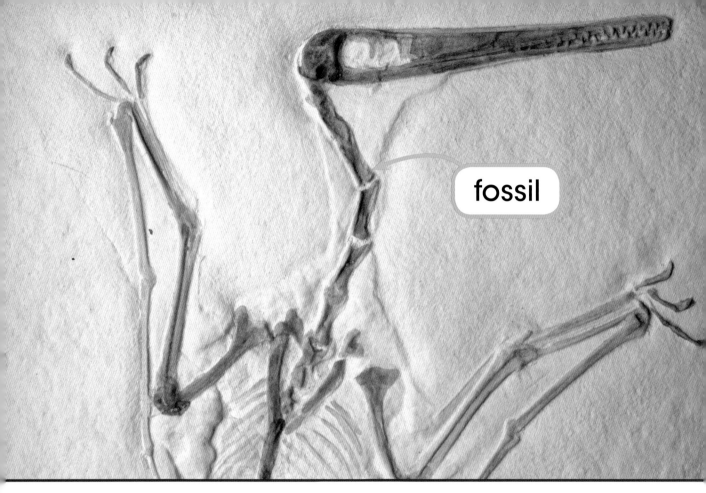

fossil

We learn about pterodactyls from fossils.

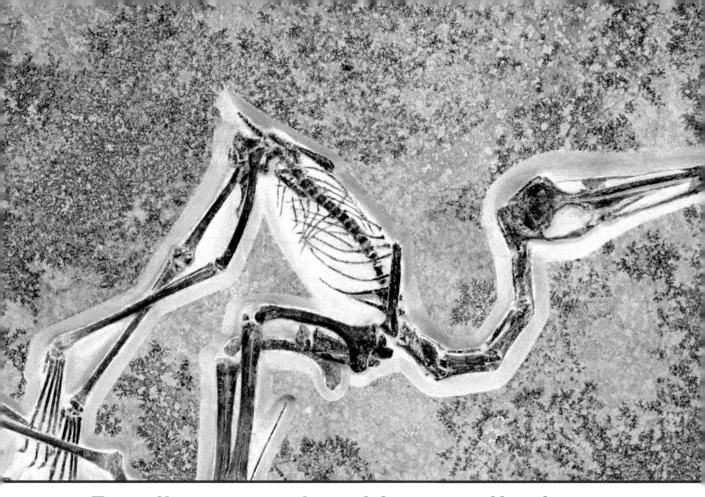

Fossils are animal bones that
have turned to rock.

People find fossils in the ground.

Fossils show us what pterodactyls looked like.

Where in the world?

Pterodactyl fossils have
been found all over the world.

Picture glossary

 **fossil** animal bones or parts of a plant that have turned into rock

 **reptile** cold-blooded animal. A lizard is a reptile.

How to say it

Pteranodon: say 'terr-arn-uh-don'

Pterodactyl: say 'terr-uh-dak-til'

Pterodactylus: say 'terr-uh-dak-til-us'

Index

Notes for parents and teachers

Before reading

Ask the children to name some dinosaurs. Ask them if dinosaurs are around today. Have they heard of pterodactyls? Explain that pterodactyls were not dinosaurs but they lived at the same time. Find out if they already know about pterodactyls.

After reading

- Choose some fast music and ask the children to fly like pterodactyls. Show them how to flap their arms and then hold them still as they glide. Ask the children to imagine they are diving to catch a fish. Then ask them to walk like a pterodactyl on the land.

- Ask the children to draw pterodactyls flying with outstretched wings. Get them to cut out their drawings and hang them from the classroom ceiling so they fly above the children's heads.